1 MONTH OF
FREE
READING

at

www.ForgottenBooks.com

By purchasing this book you are eligible for one month membership to ForgottenBooks.com, giving you unlimited access to our entire collection of over 1,000,000 titles via our web site and mobile apps.

To claim your free month visit: www.forgottenbooks.com/free967246

ISBN 978-0-260-73477-8
PIBN 10967246

Forgotten Books is a registered trademark of FB &c Ltd.
Copyright © 2018 FB &c Ltd.
FB &c Ltd, Dalton House, 60 Windsor Avenue, London, SW19 2RR.
Company number 08720141. Registered in England and Wales.

For support please visit www.forgottenbooks.com

MINUTES

—OF THE—

FORTY-THIRD ANNUAL SESSION

—OF THE—

CAPE FEAR

FREE WILL BAPTIST CONFERENCE,

HELD WITH

DUNN CHURCH, HARNETT COUNTY, N. C.

NOVEMBER 4th, 5th and 6th, 1897.

———

H. W JERNIGAN, MODERATOR; Dunn,　　　N. C.
ALEX MUNS, TREASURER, Smithfield,　　N. C.
J. F. JACKSON, SECRETARY, Timothy,　　N. C.

———

The next session will be held with Colier's Chapel Church, Cumberland County, N. C., beginning on Thursday before the 1st Sunday in November, 1898, at 12 M.

MINUTES

—OF THE—

FORTY-THIRD ANNUAL SESSION

—OF THE—

CAPE FEAR

FREE WILL BAPTIST CONFERENCE,

HELD WITH

DUNN CHURCH, HARNETT COUNTY, N. C.

NOVEMBER 4th, 5th and 6th, 1897.

———

H. W JERNIGAN, MODERATOR; Dunn,   N. C.
ALEX MUNS, TREASURER, Smithfield,   N. C.
J. F. JACKSON, SECRETARY, Timothy,   N. C.

———

The next session will be held with Colier's Chapel Church, Cumberland County, N. C.; beginning on Thursday before the 1st Sunday in November, 1898, at 12 M.

OFFICERS.

MODERATOR—H. W. JERNIGAN.
TREASURER—ALEX MUNS.
SECRETARY—J, F. JACKSON.

COMMITTEES.

ON OBITUARIES—R. C. Jackson, J. A. Hodges, and W. A. Colville.
ON MINISTERIAL CHARACTER—H. R. Hayes, C. M. Core, G. B. Strickland, W. H. Avery, and A. W. Gregory.
ON MINISTERIAL LABOR—Chairman—I. W. Taylor| Dunn, N. C., Secretary—G. B. Strickland, Smithfield, N. C. W. J. Jernigan, Alex Muns, W. P. Coher and W. A. Colville.

ORDAINED MINISTERS.

S. B. Thain	Glenmore, N. C.
Robert Strickland	" "
J. F. Hill	Goldsboro, "
Lunda Lee	Giles' Mill, "
Kenith Reynor	"
I. S. Ellis	Clayton, "
R. C. Jackson	Hawley's Store, "
J. A. Hodges	Benson, "
J. E. Smith	Myatt's Mills, "
W. R. Glover	Little River Academy, "
W. B. Hare	Manchester, "
I. F. Owen	Dunn, "
C. A. Jackson	" "
I. M. Lee	" "
J. A. Rouse	" "
Joseph Salmon	Fayetteville, "
H. W. Jernigan	Dunn, "
I. W. Lucas	" "
I. L. Ennis	Key, "
L. E. Johnson	Saulston, "

LICENTIATES.

Daniel Paircloth, J. G. Whintenton, Martin Byrd, J. C. Adams, D. R. Stafford, G. W. Jernigan, Richard Hobson, B. M. P. Coats, G. A. Pope, C. G. Hall, I. H. Faircloth, W. M. Pope, W. R. Langley, J. D. Lucas, W. H. Avery, Add Guy and Hannibal Pope.

ORDAINING COUNCIL.

Lunda Lee, R. C. Jackson and Robert Strickland.

PROCEEDINGS OF THE CAPE FEAR CONFERENCE, HELD AT DUNN, N. C.

The congregation assembles in the church at 12, M. Prayer is offered by Eld. C. A. Jackson. Owing to the absence of Eld. J. F. Hill, who was elected to preach the Introductory, and his alternate, Eld. R. C. Jackson, Eld. Lunda Lee is called to the stand and preached from 1st. Cor. 16:13, "Watch ye, stand fast in the faith, quit you like men, be strong."

After an intermission of 50 minutes, Conference reassembles and proceeds to enroll those entitled to membership.

Officers—H. W. Jernigan, Moderator; Alex Muns, Treasurer; J. F. Jackson, Secretary.

COMMITTEES.

On Obituaries—R. C. Jackson, J. A. Hodges and W. A. Colville.

Ministerial Character—W. H. Avery, A. W. Gregory, C. M. Core and G. B. Strickland.

On Ministerial Labor—H. W. Jernigan, G. B. Strickland, W. P. Colier, Alex Muns and I. W. Taylor.

Ordaining Council—Lunda Lee, R. C. Jackson and Robert Strickland.

Ordained Ministers—Lunda Lee, R. C. Jackson, J. S. Ellis, J. A. Hodges, J. E. Smith, W. R. Glover, J. H. Owen, C. A. Jackson, J. M. Lee, J. A.

Rouse, Robert Strickland, C. H. Tripp and Kenith Reynor.

Licentiate—Daniel Faircloth.

CHURCHES.

Prospect—R. M. Parker, S. L. Ennis, N. W. Colville.

Colier's Chapel—N. B. Norris, C. J. Lee, Kenith Colier.

Pleasant Grove—A. S. Lucas, W. K. Norris.

Hodges' Chapel—J. M. McLamb, Hinton Ennis.

Long Branch—Zach. Taylor, J. M. Wade, Furney Tart.

Shady Grove—E. R. Wilson, Charlie Denning.

Stoney Run—W. J. Jernigan, W. T. Barefoot, K. E. Barefoot.

New Hope—J. B. Jernigan, E. W. Marlow, J. B. Allen.

Johnston Union—J. M. Langdon, S. J. Hill, S. E. Turnage.

St. Mary's Grove—B. C. Harper, J. W. Barbour, W. J. Barbour.

Johnston's Chapel—W. H. Barbour, J. H. Stephens, J. D. Stephens.

Union Springs—J. P. Stephenson, W. H. Gregory, S. H. Davis.

Mount Pleasant—W. H. Woodall.

Wood's Grove—J. J. Roberts, J. L. Alphin, Allen Smith.

Casey's Chapel—E. E. Long, W. D. Adams.

Bethel—J. R. Massengill, E. M. Temple.

Anderson Creek—Not represented.

Hopewell-E. B. Parker, D. C. Johnson.

Dunn-I. W. Taylor, G. W. Wade, Pink Riddle.

Lee's Chapel-N. M. Eason, M. A. Williford, T. S. Tart.

Beasley's Grove-N. M. Beasley.

Lee's Grove-E. M. Tart.

Ebenezer-Not represented.

Williams' Grove-J. J. Adams, A. A. Beasley, Sandy Stewart.

Plain View-J. K. Tew, A. C. Bass.

Robert's Grove-S. F. Jackson, O. M. Jackson, V. H. Holder.

Corinth-R. H. Blue, W. F. Sewell, J. R. Phillps.

Zion-R. M. McDaniel, O. B. Warren, Ammy Godwin.

Western Conference-J. H. Worley.

South Carolina Conference-W. P. Gause.

ELECTION OF OFFICERS.

Bros H. W. Jernigan, A. W. Gregory, I. W. Taylor, R. M. Parker, and Eld. Lunda Lee are nominated for Moderator.

On second ballot Bro. Jernigan is elected by a vote of 33 to 27 against Eld. Lee.

Bros. W. H. Gregory. J. F. Jackson, A. W. Gregory and Zachary Taylor are nominated for Secretary. Jackson is declared elected by a vote of 29.

Bros. J. L. Alphin, Alex Muns and I. W. Taylor are nominated for Treasurer. Bro. Muns is elected by a vote of 35.

The Moderator calls to his assistance Eld. J. F. Owen.

The Secretary calls to his assistance Bro. A. W. Gregory.

APPOINTMENT OF COMMITTEES.

Finance—Bros. J. J. Roberts, N. B. Norris and A. S. Lucas.

Religious Exercises—Bros. J. L. Alphin, I. W. Taylor and C. M. Core

ENROLLMENT OF NEWLY ORDAINED MINISTERS.

On motion by Bro. A. S. Lucas, Eld. Jese Salmon is enrolled as an ordained minister.

ENROLLMENT OF LICENTIATES.

On motion by Eld. J. A. Hodges, Bros. J. C. Adams, J. W. Lucas, D. R. Stafford, L. E. Johnson, G. H. Jernigan, Richard Hobson, B. M. E. Coats, G. A. Pope, C. G. Hall, J. H. Faircloth, W. M. Pope, W. R. Langley, J. D. Lucas, W. H. Avery, Add Guy and Hannibal Pope are enrolled as licentiates.

Committee on Religious Exercises report to preach to-night at the M. E. church at 7:30; L. E. Johnson; at the Free Will church at 7:30, W. P. Gause

On motion, Conference adjourns to meet to-morrow at 9:30 a. m. Prayer by Eld. J. S. Ellis.

SECOND DAY.

According to adjournment, Conference is called to order by the Moderator at 9:30.

Religious Exercises are conducted by Eld. Lunda Lee.

Roll is called and 61 members answer.

Minutes of yesterday are read and approved.

Committee on Religious Exercises report to preach at the Free Will church at 11 a. m., Eld. Robert Strickland; at 2 p. m., Eld. J. S. Ellis. To night at the Free Will church at 7:30, Eld. J. F. Owen; at the Missionary church, Eld. R. C. Jackson.

The right hand of fellowship is extended to Dr. W. B. Harrel, a visiting minister from the Little River Missionary Baptist Association.

NEW CHURCHES ADMITTED.

The following are the names of the new churches admitted with delegates attached, by motion, Hickory Grove, Cumberland county; delegates—Bros. J. H. Horne and J. H. Faircloth.

Owen Grove, Sampson county; delegates-Bros. H. Lockomy, M. Simmons and R. E. Herring.

Oak Grove, Sampson county; delegates—Bros. J. E. Warren, Lovett Warren and E. M. Tart.

Hickory Grove, Robeson county; delegates—Bros. J. S. Watson and R. B. Jackson.

St. Paul, Sampson county; delegates—Bros. Blake Warren, J. M. Britt and Edgar Dameron.

Weaver's Grove, Harnett county; delegates—Bros. W. H. Wiggins and W. J. Mitchell.

REPORTS FROM CHURCHES.

The reports from churches are read (See Statistical Tables).

After an intermission of one and a half hours

for dinner, Conference reassembles and resumes work under the head of Reports from Committee

REPORTS FROM COMMITTEES.

On motion by Eld. I W. Taylor, report of committee on Ministerial Character is adopted. (See report).

On motion by Bro. J. A. Hodges, the Moderator appoint a committee to demand the credentials of *W*. L. Godwin. The Moderator appoints on this committee Elds. Lunda Lee and R C. Jackson.

On motiod by Eld J. A. Hodges, the part of the report of Committee on Ministerial Charaacter, concerning Bro. C. H. Tripp is recommitted to the committee.

On motion by Eld. I. W. Taylor, resolution by Bro. Erasmus Lee, of 1896, and tabled by motion of Eld. Wm. Byrd until this Conference, is made the special order of to-morrow 10 a. m.

Fines of 10 cts each are collected from Bros. N. W. Colville, E. R. Wilson, G. H. Jernigan and Eld. J. H. Worley.

On motion of Bro J. J. Roberts, Conference adjourns to meet to-morrow morning at 9:30. Prayer by Eld. R. C. Jackson.

THIRD DAY.

According to adjournment Conference is called to order by the Moderator at 9:30 a. m.

Religious exercises are conducted by Eld. Joseph Salmon.

Roll is called and 108 members answer.

Minutes of yesterday are read and approved.

Committee on Religious Exercises report to preach at the Free Will church at 11 a. m., Eld. J. E. Smith; at 2 p. m. Eld. Joseph Salmon; to-night at the M. E. church at 7:30, Eld. C. A. Jackson; at the Disciple church at 7:30, Eld. J. H. Worley; at the Free Will church at 7;30, Eld. J. A. Hodges.

A fine of 10cts is collected from Bro. J. M. Mc-Lamb.

The hour of 10 having arrived the resolution by Bro. E. Lee of 1896 concerning the repealing of the resolution creating a committee on Ministerial Labor, and tabled by motion of Eld. Wm. Byrd until this Conference, is taken from the table and discussed by Bros. H. W. Jernigan, Z. Taylor, Eld. R. C. Jackson and Bro. I. W. Taylor.

The resolution remain a law by a vote of 65 to 39.

On motion by Bro. Z Taylor, the report of committee on Ministerial Character, concerning Eld. Tripp is adopted; the Moderator appoint the committee requested in the report and that they investigate the charges against Elder Tripp, make final settlement and report to this body. The moderator appoints on this committee Elds. Lunda Lee, R. C. Jackson and Bro. J. L. Alphin.

On motion by Eld. J. A. Hodges, the resignation of Bro. H. W. Jernigan as a member and chairman of the committee on Ministerial Labor is accepted.

Bro. W. J. Jernigan is nominated and elected to fill the vacancy caused by the resignation of Bro. H. W. Jernigan by a vote of 49 to 40 against Bro. W. H. Gregory.

On motion of Eld. C. A. Jackson, Bro. F. K. Ginn, from the Central Conference, is given a seat in this body.

On motion of Bro. Z. Taylor, the Moderator appoints a committee of three consisting of Elders J. A. Hodges, Lunda Lee, and R. C. Jackson to revise the discipline and report to the next annual session of this body.

Conference adjourns for dinner, At 2 p. m.

Conference reassembles and resumes work under the head of Miscellaneous Business.

On motion by Bro. A. W. Gregory, the Moderator appoints a committee to examine Book of Records and report to the Secretary all unrepealed resolutions necessary to the government of this body in time to be printed in the minutes.

Elds. J. A. Hodges, Lunda Lee, and R. C. Jackson were appointed on the above committee.

On motion by Bro. A. W. Gregory, resolution

by Bro. I. W. Taylor is received for discussion (Resolution lost).

On motion by Eld. J. A. Hodges, resolution by Bro. J. L. Ennis is received for discussion. (Resolution lost).

On motion by Eld. J. E. Smith, resolution by Bro. J. W. Colville concerning the regulating of the work of the ministry is received for discussion. (Resolution lost).

On motion by Bro. W. H. Gregory, resolution by Bro. E. R. Wilson is received for discussion. (Resolution lost).

On motion by Bro. W. H. Gregory, resolution by Eld. J. A. Hodges is received for discussion. (Resolution lost).

On motion by Eld. J. E. Smith, resolution offered by Bro. B. M. F. Coats be tabled. (Motion carried).

Reports from ministers are received. (See Reports).

On motion by Bro. D. R. Stafford, the Moderator appoints a committee to sell and dispose of New Chapel church and the land, if in a condition to be sold and report this action to the next annual sitting of this body. (Motion carried).

The Moderator appoints on this committee Elds. J. A. Hodges, J. S. Ellis and Bro. D. R. Stafford.

By vote, the next session of this body is to be held with the church at Colier's Chapel, Cumberland Co., N. C.

Eld. J. F. Owen is elected to preach the introductory and Eld. J. M. Lee his alternate.

On motion by Bro. W. H. Gregory, a vote of thanks is tendered the brethren of the M. E., Disciple, Presbyterian and Missionary Baptist churches, the town of Dunn and surrounding community for kindness and hospitality shown this body during this session of Conference.

On motion by Bro. J. F. Jackson, the next session of the Sunday School Convention be held with New Hope church Johnston Co., N. C. (Motion carried).

On motion by Bro. Sandy Stewart, the report of committee to investigate the charges against Eld. C. H. Tripp is adopted.

The Moderator appoints Bros. J. J. Roberts, W. P. Colier and G. W. Wade a committee to demand the credentials of Bro. Tripp. Bro. Tripp deliberately refused to hand over his credentials to the committee; the committee is discharged.

A collection is taken up to pay the sexton $1.05 is received.

Committee on Religious Exercises report to preach to-morrow at 11 a. m. at the Free Will Baptist church Eld J. H. Worley followed by Eld. Lunda Lee; at 11 a. m. at the Presbytrian church, Elds. C. A. Jackson and W. P. Gause.

NIGHT SESSION.

Conference is called to order by the Moderator.

Prayer is offered by Eld. W. P. Gause. A fine of 10cts is collected from Bro. J. B. Allen.

On motion by Eld. R. C. Jackson, the Secretary prepares the manuscript of the proceedings of this Conference and send it to the Free Will Baptist Pub. Co., Ayden, N. C. for publication, with a request that the Pub. Co. give us a better minute than last year.

On motion by Eld. R. C. Jackson, the Secetary is ordered to have 750 copies of the proceedings of this body printed and distribute them as follows; S. C. Conference 25: Western Conference 25: Central Conference 25· Eastern Conference 25: and the balance among the churches composing this body in proportion to the amount of money paid for minutes.

On motion by Bro J. J. Roberts, Eld. R. C. Jackson is appointed as a delegate to the S. C. Conference to be held with the church at High Hill, Wiliamsburg Co , S. C. on Thursday before the 4th Sunday in October, 1898.

On motion by Eld. R. C. Jackson, the report of the Finance committee is received and committee discharged. (See report).

On motion by Eld. I. W. Taylor, resolution offered by Eld. R. C. Jackson is adopted. (See resolution).

On motion of Eld. R. C. Jackson, resolution by

Eld. Lunda Lee of 1894 concerning a Minister's Meeting is reported.

On motion by Bro. W. J. Jerenigan, the obituary of Eld. Wm. *Byrd* is received and the obituaries of Bro. Noel West and sister Phoely West be sent to the Free Will Baptist for publication.

On motion by Eld. R. C. Jackson, the Treasurer is ordered to pay after settling for minutes, any surplus mission and miscellaneous funds to Bro. A. W. Gregory on account by this body; amount. $7.

On motion by Eld. Jackson, the Secretary is allowed $10 for his services.

On motion by Eld. R. C. Jackson, the Secretary is ordered to draw on the treasurer for the amount necessary to defray the cost of printing and distributing the minutes.

On motion by Eld. R. C. Jackson, the report of committee on Ministerial Labor is adopted. (See report).

On motion by Bro. A. S. Lucas, Conference adjourn to meet with the church at Colier's Chapel, Cumberland Co., on Thursday before the 1st Sunday in Nov. 1898 at 12 m. Religious exercises are conducted by Eld. R. C. Jackson.

W. *H.* JERNIGAN, Mod,

J. F. OWEN, Asst.,

J. F. JACKSON, Clk.,

A. W. GREGORY, Reading Clk.

REPORTS.

W. R. Glover—Pleasant Grove.

W. B. Hare—*H*ickory Grove, Robeson Co., one Mission Work.

Lunda Lee—Mt. Pleasant and Shady Grove.

Robert Strickland—Hodges Chapel and Casey's Chaple.

J. F. *H*ill—Hopewell and Oak Grove.

Kenith Reynor—Beasley's Grove and Ebenezer.

R. C. Jackson—St. Paul, Plain View and Zion.

L. E. Johnson—Mission Work.

J. F. Owen—Owen's Grove, Colier's Chapel and Dunn.

Joseph Salmon—*H*ickory Grove, Cumberland Co., and Long Branch.

J. A. Hodges—Weaver's Grove and William's Grove.

J. S. Ellis—St. Mary's Grove and Union Springs.

J. E. Smith—Stoney Run.

C. A. Jackson—Wood's Grove, Johnston's Union, one Mission Work.

J. M. Lee—New Hope and Lee's Chapel.

J. A. Rouse—Lee's Grove and Bethel.

H. W. Jernigan—Prospect, Robert's Grove and Corinth.

John W. Lucas–Andersons Creek and Johnson's Chapel.

Vacancies filled by the Committee since last Conference

R. C. Jackson to fill vacancy caused by Bro. Tripp at Johnson's Chapel.

Robert Strickland to fill vacancy caused by Bro. Tripp at St. Mary's Grove.

J. H. Worley to fill vacancy caused by sickness and death of Bro. Byrd at Hopewell.

Lunda Lee to fill vacancy caused by sickness of Bro. Ellis at Stoney Run.

We recommend that the several licentiates assist the ministers in their work.

> I. W. TAYLOR, Chr.,
> G. B. STRICKLDND, Sec.

COMMITTEE APPOINTED TO INVESTIGATE AND SETTLE THE CHARGES AGAINST BRO. TRIPP.

We find after final investigation that Bro. Tripp will not submit to the rules and regulations of this Conference, also we demand this Conference to discontinue his name on the minutes and revoke his credentials for refusing to be subject to the laws of this body.

> Respectfully submitted.
> LUNDA LEE,
> J. L. ALPHIN,
> R. C. JACKSON,   Com.

FINANCE COMMITTEE.

We the Finance committee submit the following.

We find in the hands of the Treasurer:

For Minutes	$ 34.63
Miscellaneous funds	1.60
Missions	2.88
Fines	.60
Total	$ 39.71

Respectfully submitted

J. J. ROBERTS,
N. B. MORRIS,
A. S LUCAS,   Com.

COMMITTEE ON MINISTERIAL CHARACTER

We the committee on ministeral character report the following: We find or know nothing derogatory to the christian character or to their work in the ministry of any of the ministers except Bro. W. L. Godwin who has been expelled by his ch irch. We therefore, ask this Conference to demand his credentials.

Also we find that Bro. C. H. Tripp claims that the preachers of this Conference are unsettled upon the doctrine and that he will not serve the churches until the doctrine question is settled.

Also we prefer charges against him for being at variance with and accusing, brethren of lying

and says that he will not submit to serve the
caurches under the committee of apportioning
the work.

We therefore charge him with disobedience to
the sense and laws of this conference. And so
he charges our ministers of heresy by accusing
all the ministers of preaching a doctrine not in
accordance with the Bible and Discipline. We
therefore ask that this conference elect a committee to revoke and demand his credentials

C. M. CORE,

W. H. AVERY,

A. W. GREGORY,

G. B. STRICKLAND, Com.

ORDAINING COUNCIL.

We the Ordaining Council of the Cape Fear
conference submit the following report: At
Dunn N. C. during the regular session of the
annual conference, Bros. J. W. Lucas, L. E. Johnson, H. W. Jernigan and J. L. Ennis presented
themselves to council for ordination and passed
satisfactory examinations on the principles and
droctrines of the Bible and usages of the Freewill
Baptist teachings.

We therefore proceeded to ordain them after
the usual custom, a prayer charge and the lay-
ing on of the hands of the Presbytery.

LUNDA LEE,

R. C. JACKSON,

R. STRICKLAND, Ordaining Council

RESOLUTIONS.

Standing resolutions passed during the session of 1897.

RESOLUTION BY N. W. COLVILLE.

Believing that the interest of the churches demand, and in order to extend the bounds of the conference.

Therefore be it Resolved: That a new committee be elected at each session of this conference who shall regulate the work of the ministry for one year following their election.

RESOLUTION BY R. C. JACKSON.

Resolved 1st, That this conference set apart Saturday before the 5th Sunday in July or Aug. of each year in the town of Dunn, a ministers meeting for the special benefit of ministers.

Resolved 2nd, That any minister failing to attend said meeting without being providentially hindered shall not be considered in good standing.

The following resolutions were gotten up from the Book of Records by Elds. Lunda Lee, J. A. Hodges and R. C. Jackson, a committee appointed by the Moderator. They are for the guidance of the Conference and churches at large.

The committee went back to the date of 1880 and selected such laws as have been made by the Conference since that date to the present which should be obeyed,—Secretary.

RESOLUTION BY A. W. GREGORY 1890.

Resolved, That after the ensuing year closes no minister's name shall be continued upon the minutes of the Cape Fear Conference unless he present himself at each annual Conference either in person or by letter.

RESOLUTION BY ELDER JOHN MOORE 1894 AS
AMENDED BY ELDER WM. BYRD

Resolved, That a committee of five lay members of the Cape Fear Conference be appointed to have an over-sight of the character of the ministers of this Conference and that said committee report at each annual Conference,

Amendment—That the committee shall constitute apart of said Conference.

RESOLUTION BY ELDER LUNDA LEE 1893.

Seeing the necessity of a better system of Sabbath school work Be it therefore resolved

1st. That this Conference organize a Sabbath School Convention to be on Saturday before the 1st, Sunday in Oct. of each year.

2nd. That this body elect the necessary officers to govern said Convention who shall remain in office until their successors are elected.

3rd. That each Sabbath School is entitled to one representative, whose duty it shall be to carry a report of his school.

4th. That a condensed report of said convention be made yearly on our minutes.

5th. That visiting classes be made welcome in said convention.

RESOLUTION BY A. W. GREGORY 1893.

Resolved, That the church letters state to each annual Conference the number of male and female members in their respective churches.

RESOLUTION BY I. W. TAYLOR 1895

Whereas the present system of churches in regard to the work of the ministry is insufficient, therefore be it

Resolved, 1st. That this Conference appoint a committee of five of its members to assign the work of the ministry to the churches composing this Conference.

Resolved, 2nd. That the Clerk of each church in the Conference is requested to correspond with the chairman of this committee immediately after the second appointment of the pastor assigned that church and inform him whether or not the church is having preaching.

Resolved, 3rd. That said committee shall have power to investigate any rumor or general report against any minister and remove him from any work assigned him and report same to the next annual Conference for final action, and fill any vacancies.

Resolved, 4th. That all laws and clausses of

laws in conflict with this act, be and the same is hereby repealed.

Resolved, 5th. That these resolutions shall be in force from and after their ratification.

ORDER OF BUSINESS FOR 1898.

1st. Introductory Sermon, by Eld. J. F. Owen.

2nd. Enrollment of those entitled to membership.

3rd. Organization.

4th. Enrollment of newly Ordained Ministers.

5th. Enrollment of Licentiates.

6th. Call for Petitionary Letters.

7th, Appointment of Committees.

8th. Hand of Fellowship to Visiting Brethren·

9th Reports from Churches.

10th. Resolutions.

11th. Reports from Committees.

12th. Miscellaneous Business.

13th. Adjournment.

CONSTITUION.

ARTICLE 1. This body shall be known as the Cape Fear Free Will Baptist Conference.

ART. 2. The object of this Conference shall be to promote Christ's kingdom among men, by means in strict conformity to the Holy Scriptures.

ART. 3. This Conference shall be composed of its own officers, of the ministers who are members of the churches belonging to the body, of

delegates from the churches, each church being
entitled to three delegates, and one representative from each Board and Standing Committee.

ART. 4. The delegates from each church shall
bear to the Conference a letter certifying their
appointment, showing the condition and statis-
tics of the church, and giving a statement of all
funds raised during the year for denominational
or other benevolent purposes.

ART. 5 The officers of this body shall be a
Moderator, Treasurer. Corresponding and Re-
cording Secretary, who shall remain in office until their successors are elected.

ART. 6. This Conference may, at each regular meeting,
elect as many boards or standing committees as may be
necessary in carrying out its benevolent purposes.
These shall keep a reco d ot their proceedings and make
a report at each regular meeting of this Conference.

ART. 7. Any church desiring to become a member of
this body shall present her petition at a regular session
of Conference through delegates appointed for that
purpose. If she be received, the Moderator shall extend
to her delegates the hand of fellowship.

ART. 8. The Conference may extend to visiting brethren all the privileges of the body, save that of voting.

ART. 9. This Constitution may be amended at any regular session by a vote of fourfifths of the members present

OBITUARY OF ELD. WILLIAM BYRD,

Eld. William Byrd, our beloved and deceased Bro. in Christ, was born in the year of 1830, and departed this life August 30th, 1897.

He united with the Free Will Baptist church at Prospect, in the year of 1856. Soon after he was converted he claimed to have been called to preach the Gospel, in which he proved to be true in after years by being such a wonderful power in promulgating the Word of Eternal Truth. Upon his extraordinary talent in handling the Word of God while quite a babe in Christ, at his demand of the church of which he was a member, for license to preach, the church unhesitatingly granted his request. From thence forward he did a great work in the Master's cause. His preaching dates almost as far back as the Cape Fear Conference. While the Conference was in its infancy, he was a man wonderfully used of God, in turning the people from darkness to light, and from the power of satan, unto God. He also established and organized several churches during his ministerial life. His manner of preaching was wholesome and actually food for the soul of those that heard him preach. For many years he tried the fleece, both wet and dry. He was possessed of almost an ironclad resolution to meet his appointments—cold or hot, sleet or snow. It seemed to be his chief glory to do the Master's will; and though so great a worker in the Master's cause yet, like Paul, of old, when necessity was laid upon him, he refused not to labor with his own hands. And though he was a preacher of righteousness, yet he was an industrious man.

In connection with his great talent for preaching, he was possessed with the finest kind of talent for vocal music, and was known all over North Carolina as an extraordinary songster. He taught singing schools for churches of other denominations as well as that of his own. He was no respector of persons, and was very successful in cultivating a feeling of sympathy upon the part of all whom he became acquainted with. He never knew what it was to be spurned by many of his fellow men.

The writer was in conversation with the aged Elder not long before his death and he kindly gave me a short history of his life. He said: "Brother, my experience is a broad one while in life, more especially since I got into the ministry. Though I have been very successful, yet I have made some mistakes. After I was a member of the Cape Fear Conference for a number of years, under a certain persuasion I left the Conference, which I have often regretted."

During the second year of the writer's pastoral care of Prospect church, of which the Elder

was formally a member, he came out one Saturday at one of our regular quarterly meetings.
After the business of the church had all been dis-
pensed with, Elder Byrd, who at that time was
a member of the Methodist church, slowly arose
from his seat and asked permission to say a few
words. In those words he referred the church
to the past record of his life and said: "Brethren
I'm no stranger among you; for a certain persuasion, at my request, you discontinued my
name from your church roll. I now confess that
I want, by an action of this body, to come back
as a brother among you. All things work to-
gether for good to those that love God. I feel
that the mistake I have made has only served
as a means of grace in bringing me into closer
communion with my God."

Upon his noble confession he was unanimously
received back into full fellowship with Prospect
church, of which he died a member. The last
days of his life seemed to have been his happiest
ones. In the annual session of the Cape Fear
Conference in 1896, held with New Hope church,
Johnston county, Eld. Byrd preached the introductory sermon—Text: 1 Tim. 4:12. "Let no
man despise thy youth, but be thou an example
unto the believer, in word, in conversation, in
charity, in spirit, in faith, in purity." The in-
struction he gave upon this noble subject should

ever be heeded by all who heard it. Holiness and purity was the theme of his noble sermon. Soon afterwards he became a great sufferer with Bright's disease. and though the best of medical aid was obtained and the prayers of many Christians for his recovery, yet as Paul says Heb. 9:27 "It is appointed once for man to die and after that the judgment." So after many years of toil and tribulation, crosses and trials of life, the grim monster took him away from his dear companion and children, and a large circle of brethren, sisters and friends.

He was buried with Masonic honor at Pleasant Plains' church, Harnett Co., N. C. His funeral was preached by Eld. R. C. Jackson, the 3rd Sunday in October, 1897, in the presence of a large congregation

In the death of Eld. Byrd the Cape Fear Conference has sustained a loss that can never be filled, but we hope our loss is his eternal gain. "Blessed are the dead that die in the Lord."

> Farewell Brother, deep and lowly,
> Rest thee on thy bed of clay;
> Kindred spirits, angels holy,,
> Bear thy heavenward soul away.

> R. C. JACKSON,
> J. A. HODGES,
> W. A. COLVILLE, Com.

SABBATH SCHOOL REPORT.

Name of School.	Superintendent.	Members on Roll.	Number of members belonging to church.	N joioned church from S. S.	Paid for literature.	Average attendance.	Miscellaneous fund
Oak Grove............	G. *H.* Keen............	75	32	16	1 75	42	$10 93
Maple Grove........	*I.* L. Wooten..........	158	75		70	89	20 20
Shady Grnve........	A. H. Godwin..........	140	80	1	73	63	10 00
Robert's Grove......	I. L. Jackson..........	87	47	2	1 10	51	7 28
Prospect................	J. L. Byrd................	119	121		1320		

The next session will be held with the church at New Hope, Johnston Co., on Saturday before the 1st Sunday in Oct. 1898.

W. A. JACKSON Pres,

C. L. AVERY Asst,

PASTOR'S REPORTS.

Ministers.	Churches Served.	Members Received.	Sermons Preached.	Funerals.	S. S. Lectures.	Married.	Days in Revivals.	Churches Organi'd.	Amount Received.	Deacons Ordained.
J. M. Lee	2	8				2	16		$22.00	
I. A. Rouse		1	37						4.50	
J. E. Smith				4			4/8			
Kenith Reynor				4					4.50	
I. S. Ellis		8								
J. A. Hodges	3	56					6	1	32.12	
J. F. Hill	3	73	100				6	2	79.25	8
W. B. Hair			51				7			
Robert Strickland	3	16	0	3			15		32.10	
J. F. Owen	2	49	1 6			2	60	2	30.00	
C. A. Jackson	3	40							79.35	
R. C. Jackson	4	74		1					71.00	

STATISTICAL TABLE.

Churches	Counties	Pastor, '97.	Minute funds.	Paid to pastors.	Sabbath schools.	Miscellaneous funds.	Receiv'ed.	Baptized.	Excluded.	Dismissed.	Died.	No. members.	Inc ease.	Decrease.	No. males.	No. females.	Mission in lds.
rospect	Harnett	J. F. Owen	$1 00	$19 35	$14 31	$4 00	4	1	5	5	2	121	8		47	74	
odge's Chapel	"	J. E. Smith	1.30	13 35	71		14	7	8	1	1	193	3		76	117	
lesaut Grove	"	W. K. ...	1 00	23 85	1 15	4 03	13	10	3	6	2	147	2		70	77	$5 00
nderson Creek	"																
unn	"																
ee's Grove	"	R. ...	2 00	35 00			50	10	2	2	1	100	5		45	55	
benezer	"	I. A. Rouse	25	4 05			10		6	1		41		7	18	23	
illiam's Grove	"	J. A. Hodges	1 08	8 50	3 00	20 00	32	21	1			54	31		28	26	
eaver's Gove	"	J. F. Owen	25				11					11			3	8	
ong Branch	Cumberland	Ida Lee	1 20	23 80			1	1	1	1	1	127			158	69	
olier's Chapel	"	R. Strickland	1 00	30 00		14 50	14	8	1	1	1	114	12		47	67	
ickory Grove	"	Jos. Salmon	31				12	9				12					
hady Grove	Sampson	J. F. Hill	4 00	37 85	10 73		7	7	4	15	5	362		17	49	213	
toney Run	"	Lunda Lee	1 50	18 00			1	1	4		4	122		7	49	73	
ee's Chapel	"	J. F. Owen	1 10	8 20			10	5	6	2		72	1		38	34	
lain View	"	Lunda Lee	85				4	2	7			39	4		13	26	
obert's Grove	"	R. C. Jackson	1 14	16 50	8 40	300 00	16	6		2	3	52	13		25	27	
orinth	"	R. C. Jackson	90	10 86	5 42	61 09	14	8				45	14		17	28	
ion	"		16			1 00						8			5	3	60
wen's Grove	"	J. F. en	20	5 10			13	6				13			6	7	
ak Grove	"	J. F. Hill	1 00	6 25	12 68		21	18				21			9	12	
t. Paul	"	R. C. Jackson	1 00				29					29					
ew Hope	Johnston	J. M. Lee	1 75	22 00		3 50	9	7		1	1	86	8		33	53	

Church	County	Pastor													
Johnston Union	"	I. A. Hodges	1 56	8 10	1 41	12 44	8	8	2	1	1	78	4	26 52	
St. Mary's Grove	"	R. Strickland	50				2	2		4	1	25	2	9 16	
Johnston's Chap	"	R. C. Egon	1 00	20 00			3	2			1	61	2		
Union Spring	Johnston	I. A. Hodges	88	8 52		15 00	5	3	2			44	3	18 26	
Hopewell	"	J. H. Worley	1 00	12 00					4			36		4 13 23	81
Bethel	"	R. Strickland	1 00	2 10	1 30					5	1	82		6 23 57	
Beasley Grove	"	I. S. Ellis	50									56		3	
Mt. Plesant	Wake	C. A. Jackson	64	6 35	2 13	5 30	2	1	1	4		52			
Wood's Grove	Wayne	C. A. Jackson	2 00	50 00		34	19	3	3	2	140	29	50 90 2 07		
Casey's Chapel	"	I. F. Hill	1 56	24 00		14 18	2	2	2	2	2	78		4 29 49	
Hickory Grove	Robeson	W. R. Glover	50	12 4?	5 00							28			

CHURCH CLERKS WITH THEIR P. O. ADDRESS.

Prospect,   C. L. Avery,   Key,   N. C.
Hodges Chapel, J. V. Barefoot,   Benson,   "
Pleasant Grove, A. S. Lucas,   Dunn,   "
Dunn, .,   J. W. Jordan,   "   "
L. e's Grove,   Lunda Lee,   "   "
Williams' Grove, S. Stewart   Barclaysville "
W aver's Grove. J. H. Faulkner, Troyville, "
Long Branch,   L. W. Tart,   Dunn,   "
Colier's Chapel,   N. B. Norris, Carlos,   "
Hickory Grove Cumb Co. J. W. Horne   "
Shady Grove, W. A. Jackson, Hawley's store "
Roberts Grove,   O. M. Jackson,   "   "   "
Stoney Run,   W. J. Jernigan, Mingo,   "
Lee's Chapel,   N. M. Eason, .   "   "
Plain View,   J. K. Tew,   Keeners "
Corinth,   E. R. Blue,   Falcon,   "
Zion   R. M. McDaniel,   Boss,   "
Owen's Grove,   D. L. Owen, Clinton.   "
Oak Grove, E. M. Tart, Blackmon's Mills,   "
St. Paul, D. P. Dameron,   Newton Grove "
New Hope   M. F. Blackmon,   Glenmore,   "
Johnston Union, S. C. Turnage, Smithfield. "
Hopewell,   J. W. Alford,   "   "
St. Mary's Grove, B. C. Harper, Bismark, "
Johnston's Chapel J. A. Johnson,   Ezra, "
Union Springs, A. W. Gregory, Barclaysville "
Bethel,   G. H. Temple,   Four Oaks, "
Mt. Pleasant, J. D. Adams, Myatt's Mill, "
Wood's Grove,   J. J. Roberts,   Aaron, "
Hickory Grove, J. S. Watson,   Wakulla, "
Casey's Chapel,   J. F. Casey,   Elroy, "
Anderson Creek E Hair Little River Academy "